WHEN YOUR CHILD IS 6 TO 12

Other Books by John M. Drescher

Seven Things Children Need
If I Were Starting My Family Again
What Should Parents Expect?
When You Think You're in Love
Meditations for the Newly Married
If We Were Starting Our Marriage Again
Why I Am a Conscientious Objector
Spirit Fruit
Now Is the Time to Love

WHEN YOUR YOUR CHILD IS 6 TO 12

John M. Drescher

Good Books

Intercourse, PA 17534

Cover Design by Cheryl Benner
Design by Dawn J. Ranck

WHEN YOUR CHILD IS 6 TO 12
Copyright © 1993 by Good Books, Intercourse, Pennsylvania 17534
International Standard Book Number: 1-56148-094-0
Library of Congress Catalog Card Number: 93-23558

Library of Congress Cataloging-in-Publication Data
Drescher, John M.
   When your child is 6 to 12 / by John M. Drescher.
      p, cm.
   ISBN 1-56148-094-0 : $8.95
   1. Parenting. 2. Parent and child. 3. Child psychology.
I. Title.
HQ772.D684   1993
649'.124–dc20
                                              93-23558
                                                 CIP

Table of Contents

Introduction

This little book discusses a most intriguing time of childhood called middle childhood—those years when a child is ages six to twelve. We could call this period "the missing age of childhood," because these years are too seldom researched or written about. Yet these are prime years for particular preparation for adolescence and adulthood. Here is the great age of imitation when the child wants so much to be like parents and others whom the child admires, when the child will go to almost any extent to be like those who are the child's heroes. Children at this age seek to excel in areas for which they have received compliments and try to please persons whom they admire.

The burden and conviction which I bring to this book are that, while all stages of child development are significant, middle childhood is especially crucial in the development of the inner life, which prepares the child for the rest of life.

Introduction

Here the foundations are laid for the teen years. And since the middle years pass so rapidly and with relative ease because the child loves to please, parents are inclined to miss the nurturing and preparation so essential during the years six through twelve.

Much of what I share on the following pages I have discovered not only through studies, but also from exchange with many parents in retreats, as well as seminars and more specialized meetings and classes.

I give primary emphasis to children's moral and emotional development. I touch very little on their physical development.

Children have a primary need to be loved by their parents. But, in child-rearing, love is not the only prerequisite for parenthood. Understanding is a second great requirement. The child needs a love which carries a special kind of insight into the child's world, which feeds the child's spirit. This love should give the child the inner strength to build firm and healthy concepts about self and about life itself. In addition, the child needs the kind of moral guidance which gives the child a sense of responsibility and reverence, in order to make right decisions and to respect other people.

May those of you who are at the job of rearing children be helped by what you read here. May you find good hope and encouragement as you parent and prepare your children for adolescence and beyond.

—John M. Drescher

I.
Parents'
Last Great Opportunity

Middle childhood is a stage often swept over too quickly by parents and educators because it is so calm compared to the storm of adolescence. If children will ever be good, they will be good during these years. And so parents assume that all is going rather well during this time because the child, on the whole, seems cooperative, wants to please, and loves to be with the family.

It is not overstating the situation to think of this stage of childhood as "the last chance." It is the time to do many things with and for your children which you will not be able to do in the same way or to the same extent again.

Holding Your Child

"Have you hugged your child today?" is a popular slogan and bumper sticker. It is still a good question for parents. The child who does not receive daily expressions of love during the middle years will, in a few short years, reach out for love in wrong ways and to persons parents will react against in a critical way.

Middle childhood is the last good chance to hold your child close. Most children up until the ages of eleven or twelve love to be held and respond lovingly to a hug or kiss from parents. A child basks in the warmth of parental love. A child needs the assurance of being loved deeply and the security of feeling at ease in the arms of parents. An adolescent is unlikely to feel close and cared for by parents if the warmth of love and togetherness is not experienced prior to the turbulent teens.

In the middle years, the child's most important reason for wanting to be good is not fear of punishment or disapproval, but the love of parents. When love is lost or not felt, a child has little reason to be good.

This means relationships must be relaxed and comfortable. Love in the early years has a lot to do with being held close. The child must feel loved in spite of failure and even wrongdoing. Especially in times of failure and wrongdoing, love must come through.

When the child has failed, the child needs the comforting arms of loving parents. Love is most important when the child is least lovable. Even when being disciplined, the child dare not doubt the parent's love.

Over the years, as a speaker, I have had the privilege of getting into many homes. And I have learned, to some extent

10

at least, the power of touch. The Creator has placed in the heart of children the desire for closeness, for hugging, for being held, for loving. We humans—no matter our age—have been created with a desire for closeness, for hugging, for being held, for loving. In some homes I observe that it is natural for a child to sit close to the parent as we visit, with the arm of the parent around the child. It is easy to sense a feeling of genuine love flowing back and forth between parent and child.

One teenage girl explained how much her father meant to her after she had an accident during one of her first times alone in the family car. When her father arrived on the scene, he did not even look at the car; instead, he came to his daughter, found out how she was doing, and gave her a hug and kiss. "I knew," she said, "that I was precious to my father, and I knew more than ever why it is still so easy for me to feel close to my father. All through my childhood I knew that when I was in trouble, I could go to my father and feel okay again.

"During all my childhood years there was nothing I enjoyed like snuggling in my father's arms. When he held me, I felt like there was nothing in the world to fear."

All too soon the years go by, and suddenly those little ones who loved to be held close are grown and gone. Pity the parent and the child who do not take advantage of the middle years and hold each other close!

A child lives, not so much by shelter, food, or clothing, as by love. It is unconditional love which does not demand the child measure up to a particular standard in order to receive love. The parent who holds the child during the early years will have a child who will hold the parents dear in later life.

11

Spending Time With Your Child

One father discovered that his son's invitation was really a compliment. The club the boy belonged to scheduled a boat trip and his son asked him to go along. Since the dad was not a very good swimmer and he was quite busy, he began to hedge. "Get yourself a buddy," he said, "and I'll pay the bill." His son replied, "No, I don't want a buddy. I want to go with you."

That father was wise in going with his son. We need to remember that love is spelled T-I-M-E. If we do not take time with each other, we cannot grow in love.

One young father posted this notice on the refrigerator: "I will not read the newspaper or watch TV when my family is available, so that I can spend time with them."

Parents who have time to do many things with each other and with their child during middle childhood will find that they have a child who has time for its parents during its teens and later life. The parents who do not capitalize on time with their child during these significant years should not expect that the child will want them around in its adolescent years.

A small boy kept asking his dad to build a clubhouse in the backyard. The father assured him that he would help him, but each week he was involved in a business appointment, a golf date, some pressing home work, or social engagement.

One day the little fellow was hit by a car and was taken to the hospital in critical condition. As the father stood by the bedside of his seriously injured child, his son said with a smile, "Well, Dad, I guess we won't get to build that clubhouse."

Of course the boy didn't want a clubhouse as much as he wanted his dad. In middle childhood the child loves time especially with Mother and Dad. And never again will the child be so open to doing many things *together* as a family.

Middle childhood is the last good chance for children and parents to spend quality and quantity time together. In adolescence the child craves time primarily with others of the same age. During middle childhood the child loves to do things with its parents and family. And this togetherness builds feelings of belonging. But togetherness takes time—planned time and special time.

Middle childhood, therefore, is the last chance to do many things together and to go many places together. After twelve years of age the child will seek friends elsewhere, especially if parents are not the child's close friends during preadolescence.

Following World War II in Europe, there were countless war orphans. The only children who could be brought back to a sense of normalcy again were those who remembered doing many things together with their families.

Giving ourselves is not easy. It takes purpose and planning. Someone has written, "Of course it is much easier to give *things*, instead of ourselves, just as it is easier to send a card than to pay an unhurried visit."

One father, after his son was beyond the time of persuasion and punishment, said, "I planned to go out with my boy and be his companion, when I had time. I hoped to interest him in young people's activities, when I had time. I promised I would talk with him like a father should with his son, when I had time. But for over twenty years, for every one thought of my son, I had a hundred thoughts of my business."

13

Years ago the United States had an ambassador to England by the name of Adams. He took a day off to go fishing with his son. That day he wrote in his journal, "Wasted day! Went fishing with my son." His son, however, wrote later of this time as the greatest day of his life—when he "went fishing with my father."

If we as parents do not give loving attention during this stage, the child will get angry attention from us by misbehaving.

Instilling Values

By the age of thirteen, the average child is said to have asked five hundred thousand questions. This is the Creator's way of providing opportunity for our children to learn the answers to life's questions before adolescence. And during these preadolescent years, we have a chance to share our beliefs with our children. That's half a million opportunities to teach something about the meaning of life and to impart our values. These questions are all what, why, and how questions, which can stretch us beyond our own resources. These moments give us abundant opportunities to relate all of life to our basic values and outlook on life.

Middle childhood is a prime time to instill values in a child. Then the child is eager for parents to share stories of what it was like when parents were young. "Tell me about when you were a little girl or when you were a little boy" are requests that come often. In telling such stories, parents have the precious privilege to share their values of life. If you wait until the child arrives at thirteen years and beyond and then try to say, "Now when I was a little girl . . . " or "When

I was a little boy . . . ," see how quickly you are turned off! The opportunity to pass ideals along in this way is gone.

By adolescence, children know what their parents believe and think, and how their parents will respond to almost any given situation. They have either experienced a close parental relationship, or they have sensed neglect and distance, depending upon the responses which parents have made to their questions and needs. Their question at this stage is, "What will I believe and think, and how will I respond to what I have seen and heard?"

As parents, therefore, we ought to seize the opportunities both to share the lessons we have learned, and to give our child rules and standards which will guide the child in the way the child ought to go. This does not mean we continually lecture. What it does mean is that we need to take the time to listen, to answer the child's questions well, and to share our own stories and experiences which the child loves to hear over and over again. In this way we are always teaching.

One of the earliest statements about child guidance for parents is found in the Scriptures, the Old Testament book of Deuteronomy, chapter 6, verses 6-8. This passage points out that the truth of God shall first be acknowledged by parents, who are then to teach it to their children. The original meaning suggests that teaching is to be applied like a surgeon's knife, carefully placed where the need lies. It should not be just a smattering of instruction, thrown out in all directions. Neither is the application the same for each child, since each child is different and responds to love and instruction in the child's own unique way.

This passage urges parents to teach constantly—when

they sit in the house, when they are going about their work, when they lie down, and when they get up. In other words, teaching is not given only on a special day or time, nor is it done by sending the child off to school or church. Rather, the natural and most effective way to teach is through the experiences of every day. Then the child will not get the idea that faith and God are separate from real life or reserved only for church one day each week.

We teach all day long by the way we live—what we speak about, how we answer the questions of our children, by the very pictures on the walls of our houses, by the responses parents make about and to others, and by the way parents pray and commit themselves to God for the day and at the close of the day. Spiritual words have meaning to the child only as the child experiences them primarily within the family.

In his book, *A Small Town Day*, Rufus Jones tells about morning worship in his home as a child: "But there was something more to our family religion than this morning devotions together. The life in our home was saturated with the reality and practice of love . . . It was an old-fashioned home where nurture went on all the time. It was a life-building center. It was there that my anchor was forged."

Our lives as parents must be consistent with what we teach, because example will be the final confirmation of what we say.

A cub scout was elected treasurer of his group. After some time it was discovered that he was pilfering the funds. When his dad found out about his stealing, he gave his son a very severe scolding, only to have his son, in all honesty, reply, "But Dad, that was only five dollars. I heard you say the other day that you beat the government out of five hundred dollars in income tax."

Never again will parents have a better opportunity to teach. It is true, of course, that parents need to continue to share their values with their children during the teen years. But then it is different. During middle childhood the *children* ask the questions for parents to answer and teach values. In adolescence the *parents* need to ask questions which challenge their teens' thinking and ideas. But during the teen years, categorical statements or categorical answers are despised.

Reading to Your Child

Children in their middle years find reading to be one of their favorite activities. And they love to be read to. Here is our last opportunity to have our children snuggle close and to influence their reading of worthy books which can build true values and challenge them to worthy goals and purposes. During these years especially, they love biographies and autobiographies of great persons, as well as stories of children who proved true under trying situations. Children are caught up by stories of persons who display great virtues and who are worthy of admiration. Such stories shape the children's thinking and desire for the pure, the noble, and the true. Heroes are very important for children during this age—heroes of conviction, courage, and honor. And if parents do not provide heroes, children will find their own heroes of one kind or another.

It is at this point that parents can both read good books to their child and have good books, magazines, and other reading materials available for the child. Without these, a child is likely to be drawn away to the shallow and hurtful influence of TV, and to worthless or even harmful reading material that is within easy reach.

Because reading is such a favorite activity during these years, parents can do more than provide plenty of proper reading material; they can also read to the child and discuss what they have read together. The privilege of discussing with one's child the essential goals and ideals of life will be gone, to a large degree, in a few years.

This is also a prime time for traveling to and visiting significant places and people. Both will leave lasting impressions on a child of this age.

Now is the time to discuss issues of morality and to tell stories of how it pays to live good moral lives. One father said his children never seemed to be attracted to drugs and alcohol because their entire family went regularly to assist in ministering to those affected by these evils.

It is particularly important to read to the child stories which build emotional warmth, caring, and love, because it is through *feelings* that the child identifies, even more than through facts. Through emotions the child makes application to life, more than through careful reasoning. I cannot stress too much that the feelings generated through reading and contact with parents will guide and bless the child during the rest of life.

Bedtime is a good time to read to a child. It seems that God has put within children a hesitancy to go to bed, so that parents, if they will, can have a special time at the close of the day to spend with their children. We are told that a child awakens with much the same spirit the child had when going to sleep. Here is a great privilege and opportunity to not only give needed guidance, but also to meet the child's basic emotional need to love and to be loved.

Teaching the Facts of Sex

Middle childhood is the primary time to discuss sex freely and to talk about the issues involved in dating, courtship, and marriage. All the facts of sex should be shared before adolescence. It is now that the child can learn and accept all the facts of sex without emotional overtones or embarrassment. Wait until the child reaches thirteen years and beyond, and the child will get red in the face and want to get away. Parents also find it more difficult to discuss sex during adolescence because of the emotional feelings of the child.

A child who enters adolescence knowing the facts of sex can hear all the crazy stories and misinformation-information that floats around showers, rest rooms, and halls at school and can say, "I know better than that. My parents told me." Such a child is prepared to face adolescence with a security, a stability, and a sense of life's sacredness that is needed in the teen years.

We usually begin four to six years too late in giving our children specific guidance in dating, courtship, and marriage. It's rather difficult to give instructions for dating to a teenager in the heat of that experience. It isn't easy to try to set standards for boy-girl relationships for teens who are sure parents' ideas are centuries behind the time. Standards are instilled very early.

A mother told me a story that begins when her daughter

was in the early years of middle childhood, playing with her dolls. She decided to dress her dolls up for a date and called to her mother, "How old are people when they date?" "Oh," her mother replied, "they should be at least sixteen."

Years went by, and the daughter, now nearly sixteen years of age, was asked out for a date. She refused. She told her mother, who was quite impressed with the young man who asked her daughter for a date, and who implied that the young woman could have gone out with him. "But," said her daughter, "you don't want to go back on your own principles, do you?" It was then that this mother realized how early we begin teaching and how important that early teaching really is.

When, then, is the time to prepare? It is clear that we need to do our preparation in these areas during middle childhood. Simply begin by answering the child's questions regarding sexual organs and reproduction in an honest and open way. During these years, the child feels a special closeness and love for parents who explain the basic facts of sex and life. The child develops a strong sense of belonging, of oneness, and of being cared for when parents talk about all these concerns.

What better way to build confidence and endearment for each other than to share at this level! Yes, the child needs to know the facts of life, but, far beyond these, the child needs to have the experience of a parent's trust, love, and care, which become evident during this kind of preparation for what is ahead.

If parents talk in this way with a child during the middle childhood years, the child will also feel more free to express to parents the puzzling feelings and frustrations of the teen years later on. But if parents do not relate at these levels during middle childhood, they should hardly expect their child to relate at any depth during adolescence.

One father talked with his ten-year-old daughter about the facts of reproduction, boy-girl relationships, and the right and wrong uses of our God-given sexual drives. After this close and caring discussion he said to his young daughter, "Today I am going to give you a dime [it was sufficient at that time]. If any time in your dating experience a young man should ask you to engage in sex, go to the nearest telephone and call me. I'll be there for you immediately."

That daughter grew into a teenager and young adult. She dated a fine young man, and one day they were married. The first night of their honeymoon her father received a call. "Dad," his daughter said with a touch of humor. "You remember I promised to call you if ever a young man proposed we engage in sex. So I thought I'd give you a call tonight. Thanks Dad, we are doing fine."

Think of what that talk meant to that young girl in preparing her for a happy courtship and marriage! And think of how so simple a thing as a dime reminded that young woman of the purity of life all through her teens into marriage itself.

Here, then, are several examples of "last things" we can do naturally with our children during their middle childhood years. These are the years of great possibilities for closeness, communication, and counsel. If we miss these opportunities to relate to and respond in the proper way with our child, the years ahead will be difficult ones. But if we seize these years when the child loves and longs for closeness with parents, the pattern is also set for closeness in the future years.

2.
Characteristics
of Middle Childhood

Rather than discussing all of the unique characteristics of the preadolescent, I will focus on those traits having to do with the further development of the child's conscience and acceptable behavior.

A Latency Period

By and large, these years are a time of peace. They are often referred to as a "latency" period in a child's life. Because they are such, and because during this stage the child, like at no other time in life, seeks to please parents and other adults, parents may be tempted to relax too much and neglect some of their most important responsibilities and opportunities.

During this latent or dormant period, a great deal of maturing takes place. The child is like a photographic plate, absorbing pictures of everything and everyone around, and filing all away for future reference. Much of the child's development at this time is within or at the sub-surface level.

Because the child seems cooperative, parents are tempted to believe that most of their child-rearing responsibilities are now out of the way. The outward aggression expressed by the child in earlier years seems to turn into inward introspection. Conflicts seem to resolve into adjustment.

But in fact, this latency period is a prime time for parents and children to learn to know each other. In a real sense, this is the parent's last chance to play a truly full and special role as a friend, counselor, and guide. The character of the child during this time gives a strong indication of the sort of adult the child will eventually become. The quality of relationship that the child and its parents develop during this period is a sort of forecast of the kind of relationship they will experience during the child's adolescence. Here is an opportunity for parents to help their child unfold, while there is still the possibility of shaping the child.

The Need for Affection

In children's wards of hospitals, doctors often prescribed TLC—tender, loving care—for their young patients. The greatest hindrance to a growing spirit is the lack of love. We are told that some children shrivel up and die physically because of lack of love. Many more shrivel up and die emotionally because of lack of love.

This inner need to love and be loved is abundantly strong in all persons, regardless of age. The way we parents extend love to our child affects the child's ability to love and relate to others. To the degree we include our children in our lives, show our love, speak our love, and respond in love—to that extent our children become capable of including others in their love.

Dr. Wanda Walker described the results of a study of maladjusted teenagers conducted in a large Oklahoma high school. A team of counselors spent time gaining rapport and the confidence of ten of the most neglected and maladjusted children in the school. Eventually they asked them how long it was since their parents told them that they loved them. Only one remembered ever hearing it at all, and that child could not remember when.

In contrast, the counselors called out ten of the best adjusted, most well accepted, outstanding leaders of the school and asked them the same question. Without exception these answered, "This morning," "Last night," and "Yesterday." All indicated that their parents verbally expressed their love in the past twenty-four hours.

A leader in public education, speaking to school administrators, said that a lot of intelligent, capable children will not make it. They do not need stricter discipline, more skills, and better educational methods. Instead, they will not make it because they feel alienated. They need to feel that they are loved and that they belong. "So," he urged administrators and teachers, "let love shine forth from your eyes."

Some years ago a sociology class at Johns Hopkins University made a study of children in a depressed neighborhood in Baltimore. They identified two hundred children who appeared doomed to prison in adulthood.

After twenty-five years, another sociology class set out to discover what had happened to those particular people. The class found that only two of the two hundred had been in prison.

As they interviewed these men and women they found that the sociology class had been right. They were headed for prison. By all indicators and predictions they were destined to a life of crime.

But something unpredictable happened. The interviewers, this time around, heard one name again and again—Aunt Hannah. Aunt Hannah, an elementary school teacher, made the difference. She taught and loved those troubled children from bad homes and bad communities. And because she loved them they became responsible adults. Aunt Hannah changed the direction of the lives of a generation in that community.

Certainly Aunt Hannah must have accumulated her share of scars as God loved and changed these lives through her. George Eliot was right: "Blessed is the influence of one true, loving human soul on another."

We cannot change the color of a child's eyes but we can give the eyes the light of understanding and sympathy. We cannot alter a child's features, but we can, in many ways, endow the child with the glow of humanness, kindness, and friendliness. And all of that will, in the long run, bring a lot more happiness than the perfection that wins beauty contests. We cannot give security by surrounding a child with an abundance of things, but we can give the real security the child needs by enclosing the child in the arms of our love.

It is not overstating the situation to claim that at this middle stage of childhood, a child's most important reason for wanting to be good is because the child senses the love of its parents. When that love is lost or not felt, the child has little reason to be good. The child lives by love more than by shelter, food, clothing, or toys.

Marshall F. Mauney tells a story about a boy who climbed high into a tree and refused to come down. Throughout dinner, which his parents ate with exaggerated relish in the boy's view, remarking frequently and fatuously upon the particular delights of the meal, the boy clung stubbornly to his limb, far too high for his father to climb after him.

They tried everything, the mother whined frantically to the doctor hours later over the telephone. "Everything" meant threats, bribery, cajolery, lies, warnings, and screams. "We told him he'd fall and hurt himself. We told him we'd call the fire department, and the firemen would say what a baby he was. We told him he'd catch cold and get sick. We told him there were owls in the tree that would peck his eyes out. We told him he'd get thrashed within an inch of his life if he didn't come down. We've tried everything."

"Did you tell him simply that you wanted him to come down because you loved him and wanted him to be with you?" the doctor asked. "Well, no," she said. She called back a few minutes later to say that the boy, who seemed to have been waiting for five hours to hear just that, had come right down.

Psychiatrist Ross Campbell, in *How To Really Love Your*

Child, says, "In all my reading and experience I've never known of one sexually disoriented person who had a warm, loving, and affectionate father." Psychologists tell us that many men are victims of the "taboo of tenderness." Let it be said loud and clear that the truly strong are tender, the truly great are gentle, and the truly wise are warm and loving.

Love means taking time for and with your child. A significant Christmas or birthday gift from a parent to a child would be, "This next year I promise to give you one-half hour each day and a special time together each week."

Listening is a mark of love. In fact, listening and loving are twins. Children want and need undivided attention. Parents who listen to their child when the child talks will have a child who will demand less time in the long run. Parents who listen to their child when the child is young will have a child who will be inclined to listen to the parents when the child is older.

Evelyn Millis Duvall in her fine book, *Handbook For Parents*, highlights the primary responsibility parents have to keep their own love life strong because of the effect it has upon the child. She writes, "It is at this point that child development specialists and students of family life concur that the central relationship in the home must be the husband and wife axis and not the parent-child tie. The child cannot be expected to bear the burden of parents' frustrations and adult hungers. It is only when husband and wife meet one another's needs in satisfying ways that they are free themselves for wholesome love for their children. Such a marriage is the true heart of the home and the wellspring of caring for children in optimal ways. Even the one-parent family must find ways of safeguarding the children from the single parent's affectional needs."[1]

Psychiatrist Justis S. Green says, "In my twenty-five years of practice I have yet to see one serious emotional problem in the child whose parents loved each other or whose love for the child was an outgrowth of their love."

When parents love each other, and when that love is felt and seen, it gives a security, stability, and sacredness to life which a child can learn in no other way. When love between mother and father is not felt and is not demonstrated, the child is likely to pick up all kinds of distorted ideas about love and life.

Dr. David Goodman writing to parents says, "Your baby will smile at you and later at the world if you two never cease smiling at each other. No fact of child training is truer or more important than this." It is good to remember that parenthood is passing; partnership is permanent. So keep the partnership in good repair and parenting will be more likely to take good care of itself.

If parents walk hand in hand, the child is quick to join hands. When parents express genuine love, the child will grow in love. If parents build their own relationship, the child reaps the benefits and blessings of that love.

When a child knows its parents love each other, hears words of love, and sees acts of love, the child needs little explanation of God's love, human love, or the sanctity of sex. But if the child does not feel, hear, or see that love, if it is not demonstrated between father and mother, the child will have its perception of love shaped by friends, TV, movies, and other relationships it observes.

A word of warning. A child finds hidden hostility very difficult to bear. A child will go to pieces emotionally, sooner or later, when the child senses something is wrong between its father and mother, and yet it is hidden. While the child can deal with a great amount of open disagreement and argument between parents if they also express love for each other, the child is unable to stand the strain which arises out of the coldness and cruelty of hidden hostility between its parents.

Pity the child who has never seen open disagreement. Such a child enters later life and marriage with a false concept of real life. Pity the child, as well, who does not see reconciliation and love expressed after conflict. Such a person can hardly learn the meaning of forgiveness and love, nor how to resolve difficulties.

The Child's Emotional Growth

During the years six to twelve, the child's emotional and cognitive development is happening quickly and in concert. Not only does the child remember the facts of what happened, the child is equally able to recall the feelings accompanying a situation—a trip, an accident, or a visit. Both register at this age—the details of how long the journey or how serious the hurt or what was said or done—as well as how it all felt.

The child tends to remember and sense emotions from an experience, perhaps more than precise teachings, and is as alert to *how* and in *what tone* something is said, as to *what* is said. The child is likely to remember with exactness its inner emotional responses as much as what happened physically.

This means that to talk to or teach a child with respect, love, kindness, and affection helps the child to feel good about the child's own well-being, ability, and self-image.

The best teaching will likely be ignored or rejected if that teaching is not given in a caring and loving spirit. This is why a child who is taught a great deal of ethical or moral behavior may sometimes seem to reject it.

For the teaching to be received internally, a child's feelings must become involved. Regardless of how good the teaching may be, if the atmosphere or attitude during the teaching is unpleasant, the feelings become more determinative than the teachings.

Many years ago Francis S. de Fenelon wrote, "If virtue offers itself to the child under a melancholy and constrained aspect, while liberty and license present themselves under an agreeable form, all is lost, and your labor is in vain." Therefore, if we are to care for the child ethically, morally, or spiritually, we must care for the child emotionally. Pleasant memories must accompany the facts and lessons we wish to teach or the teaching will prove ineffective.

When I was a child of ten, a good friend of our family took special interest and time with several of us boys, ranging from ages ten through twelve. The gracious woman read entire books to us—stories of heroes and moving stories of persons who faced tremendous difficulties and proved brave and true.

While I do not recall much about the stories, not even the titles of the books, I do remember this dear woman sometimes getting out her handkerchief and wiping her tears because she herself was so moved by these stories. Never will I forget her deep feelings, her concern for persons, her love for truth, her ability to identify with the trials and also the triumphs of persons. My own boyhood emotions identified with the true and noble, the compassion and the character of one who cared so deeply for people.

The Need for Encouragement

"When I was eight years old, I was playing in the house and singing some of the songs I learned in school. My mother came into my room and said 'You have a wonderful singing voice.' I went on to become a music major and taught music all my life." A woman in Illinois told me this about her own life after I had spoken about the need for encouragement.

In the child's development from newborn to toddler, to pre-schooler and then to school-age, the parent's role changes from care-giver, to protector, to nurturer, and then to encourager. The child at this age blossoms under encouragement. We say the child at this age will "break his or her neck" to please the parent.

Even though peer conformity does show itself during these early years of school, it does not seem to increase parent-peer conflict to any marked degree. Rather, children have alternative and additional sources of rewards and evaluations in school life. With school comes the simultaneous presence of peers and anxieties about failure and rejection in relationships. Consequently, the role of parents as encouragers becomes crucial.

Further, studies are clear that encouragement seems to be the best corrective influence on behavior during this period. As interaction between parent and child becomes more psychological and less physical, and as children are exposed to a wider range of significant other persons and experiences, the parent's primary role becomes more and more that of encourager.

Discipline during these middle childhood years is most

effective if parents give the reasons for desirable behavior, clearly explaining how that behavior affects oneself and others. It is certainly appropriate to continue to set limits for children of this age, since they are increasingly capable of understanding such expectations. Above all, however, it is important to convey an attitude of encouragement rather than punishment since the child is especially responsive to the slightest word or act of encouragement.

Of course, at this stage, a primary goal for parents is to promote their children's self-respect while gradually encouraging their greater independence and self-discipline.

Active and Noisy

A healthy, happy preadolescent is an active, noisy youngster who finds it hard to sit still. These children will practice endlessly at developing their skills in sports, music, and other areas which fascinate them at the moment. All of that is good and appropriate since the child, in this way, develops self-confidence and discovers its particular interests.

During this stage the child becomes immersed in hobbies, the kind of activity that builds a child's sense of adequacy. Children benefit immensely by receiving wholehearted parental support of their projects. Parents who show interest bolster their child's sense of self-worth significantly.

When children are affirmed, they develop great interest in their projects and become diligent, preparing for the time in adolescence when they are likely to be plagued with feelings of inadequacy and inferiority.

A Sense of Industry and Competence

During these years the child is filled with energy, inquisitiveness, and the desire to do things. It is now that attitudes toward work, work habits, competence, and abilities in special areas of interest are being formed. This is the time for parents and teachers to promote all kinds of opportunities and experiences for the child to succeed. This is the stage when habits are being formed which will reach through the rest of life.

During middle childhood the child works without ceasing to develop mentally and physically. The child's knowledge of the world is expanding and, with that, an interest in how things are made and how they work.

It is the age of all kinds of "collections, "projects," and "messes." The child, if encouraged, and, particularly, if joined by parents, grows in both responsibility and competence. And when the child's use of expanding skills and abilities meets with success and the child receives support, appreciation, and approval of parents, peers, and teachers, the child develops a sense of industry. In addition, the child becomes dependable. Studies show that a surprising number of persons decided on a future occupation during their middle childhood years because they received an affirming word from someone at this most responsive time.

On the other hand, if the child at this great age of "doing" receives criticism, has repeated experiences of failure, and is not complimented and encouraged, the child will live with a sense of incompetence and inferiority. This age child can readily carry many fears of inferiority when trying new things.

Benjamin West described how he became a painter. One day his mother needed to make a quick trip to the grocery store and left him with his sister Sally. While she was gone, he found colored ink in the cupboard and began to paint his sister's portrait. When his mother returned, she ignored the ink spattered over the table, leaned over his shoulder and exclaimed, "Why, that's Sally," and gave him a kiss. Benjamin West said, "My mother's kiss that day made me a painter."

Walter Scott, as a child, was considered a dullard. He was made to sit alone in the corner of the classroom many times. However, one evening his parents were entertaining several famous literary characters in their home. Among them was the well-known Robert Burns who noticed a picture on the wall with a couplet from a poem. He asked who wrote the poem, but no one seemed to know. Then the timid Walter Scott walked to his side, told him who wrote the poem, and repeated the rest of the stanza. Burns placed his hand on the head of Scott and said, "Ah, barnie, thou wilt be a great man in Scotland some day." History says from that time Walter Scott was a different boy. And in years to come he became known around the world as Sir Walter Scott.

Of course play continues to be important in building a child's sense of competence and self-worth. A child who is put under pressure to perform perfectly is likely to develop great feelings of inadequacy and incompetence. In fact, the competitive aspect of organized sports can easily overshadow their inherent teaching potential. Who has not attended Little League games that compare in stress to the World Series? The desire to win—especially on the part of parents and coaches—supersedes any effort to help children develop and refine their skills or to teach them valuable lessons of cooperation, fair play, and confidence.

Parents' and coaches' egos can become too intertwined with their children's performances. It is the parents' job to examine carefully the competitive aspect of the organized groups their children are considering joining and to be aware of their dangers. Our drive as adults to have our children be superior in their sports, their grades, and a hundred other ways, can well be the cause of our children's feelings of inferiority. While we work to fulfill our own needs, we can destroy our children's sense of industry and competence.

The Smart Age

Children from six to twelve may be keenly aware of their feelings, but they are also razor-sharp in learning facts, picking up every inaccurate statement, reacting against injustice, and often being relentlessly exacting of themselves and others. One writer says that the preadolescent child has the memory of an elephant for things that strike the child's interest. Make a promise to go fishing or attend a ball game, to buy a dress or go shopping on a certain day, and it will never be forgotten. This means that parents in particular must practice honesty and integrity if the child is to grow in these traits.

Sometimes it seems this age child loses all respect for manners. Being noisy and intellectually curious, children of this age have a great desire to do things, to be useful, and to assume responsibility. Now they shun baby ways and yearn to be needed like adults are. Parents can capitalize on these natural inclinations and help by steering their children's interests into right areas.

The Need to Belong

These children have a great urge to belong to a group, a club, or a gang of peers. Each child needs a small group of intimate friends. Girls want to be with girls and boys with boys; everyone finds it upsetting to be exiled from a group. At this age it is almost a sin to be different in any way, particularly in clothes, manners, and interests. This means that a good gang or group or club is of tremendous help in shaping a child's attitudes toward life and toward others.

Home to the preadolescent is a necessary and natural base from which to operate, but it becomes more and more a place to go when you can't go anywhere else. The preadolescent child likes to be on the go, yet needs the security of a happy home to return to.

At this time a child may sincerely miss a parent when the parent is away. On the other hand, the child may seem to overlook or ignore the parent when she or he is present. The child will loudly proclaim the virtues of a neighbor's or friend's home, yet will proudly invite those persons to his or her own home.

From where does a sense of belonging come? Doing things together gives children not only a sense of being loved, but also of belonging. Children tend not to remember the things they've done alone nearly as well as the things they do together with persons who love and respect them.

The Need to Discuss Ideas and Do Things Together

What the child especially needs during these years is to have a climate in which to express ideas freely. The child needs to air thoughts and feelings and will benefit greatly if parents use this time to learn to know and understand their child's thinking and desires. The preadolescent is quite capable of reasoning if the right kind of atmosphere prevails. Children will share to the extent they know they will continue to be loved and accepted.

This is also the time when the child becomes more inquisitive about sex and human relationships. Parents need to be prepared for questions of all kinds—questions about sex, lies, and stealing. We ought not to be caught off guard and resort to responses such as, "You're a dirty boy," or "Nice children don't talk that way," or "You are bad."

Unless we parents prepare ourselves about the meaning of this kind of behavior, we may be tempted to react or to answer too quickly. But if we make an effort to understand our child's development, as well as thinking ahead of time about how we feel about the behavior they want to discuss, we will find it easier to handle when these events take place. How we respond will also determine to a great degree how open our child will be with us during the teen years.

Remember, a child will share only to the extent the child knows he or she will continue to be loved and accepted. This is, of course, true at all levels and ages.

A Love of Adventure

Children of this age anticipate and enjoy adventure—both in play and in intellectual matters. The broader we make these horizons and the more things we provide for the child to learn to do, the better we prepare the child for a richer adolescence.

Many children are enthusiastic lovers of books at this age and can find a great deal of adventure in reading. Adventure stories which portray heroes with integrity can be very influential. Taking children to visit important places and significant persons at this stage in their lives can also leave lasting impressions.

During these few years a great deal of consolidating and maturing takes place. The "clay" is not yet hard, and adults have a chance to play a special role in shaping the child's thinking. Parents ought to take the opportunity to discuss all kinds of issues, concerns, and relationships, especially at this time.

This age child is delighted to participate in all kinds of activities with parents—an urge that changes quickly in just a few years! It is also a good time to help the child explore and develop skills in a variety of fields of interest. Everyone at this age needs to accomplish something in order to believe in oneself and to have a sense of measuring up around one's peers. Even more, the child wants to measure up to the expectation of its parents. William Jones wrote, "The deepest principle in human nature is the craving to be appreciated." Don't forget to praise your children and thereby please them in this most basic way.

The Need for Rules

If rules are of primary importance during the first few years of a child's life, they remain essential for the child from ages six through twelve. Children feel secure when rules are clear and specifically enforced. In fact, children in this age group are meticulous at playing a game by the rules. On the contrary, the child left without rules becomes ill at ease and feels unloved. Wrote the editor, Leonard Gross, "A child with unlimited freedom gets frightened; he suspects he isn't loved."

This does not mean that parents need a long list of rules; rather, it means that parents should have explained *important* rules which the child understands and is expected to follow as a member of the family. A good rule has at least three important ingredients. First, does it hurt or help oneself or others? Second, does it deal with what is morally right or wrong? And third, does it deal with those things the family, with the parents' leadership, has decided shall be the practice of all within the household?

Let us remember, however, that children obey and honor their parents, not primarily because the Bible tells them to, or because parents do everything right, but because parents love, understand, and build meaningful relationships with their children in their work, play, and daily experiences. Wise parents use discipline which increasingly puts responsibility into the hands of the child, in order to prepare the child for true maturity.

Finally, be encouraged, parents! A child's psyche is quite durable. Psychologists remind us that parents can make many mistakes, but if a basic love is present the child will develop in strength, stability, and security.

3.
Guided
by Imitation

A cartoonist pictures a puzzled father with his elbows on the dinner table. He is looking down the length of the table at his wife and complaining, "Why can't they know that it is wrong for everybody but me to sit this way?"

Walt Whitman wrote, "There was a child went forth each day. And the first object he looked upon, that object he became."

Middle childhood is a lively stage of child development because the child seeks to imitate those whom the child admires. The child's social, moral, and spiritual development moves from regulation to imitation.

During the first five years the child depends upon parents

for guidance, rules, and the setting of standards. The child who early knows what the boundaries are becomes a secure and happy child.

There was the kindergarten youngster who reported, "We had a substitute teacher today. She left us do whatever we wanted, and we didn't like her." The child who does not know where the walls are will kick and kick to feel those walls, and remains insecure and unsure. When the walls are not there, or when the walls are continually shifting, depending upon the mood of the parent, the child becomes insecure.

The Age of Imitation

Although rules continue to be important for six- to twelve-year-olds, the primary way these children are guided is more and more by imitation and less and less by regulation. If very young children are most impressed by *what* they are told, the child in the middle years is most conscious of *who* says what. The example of parents and other important persons in the life of the child is now the primary factor in the child's social, moral, and spiritual development.

John Balguy's words are never more important than now: "Whatever parent gives child good instructions, and sets them at the same time a bad example, may be considered as bringing them food in one hand and poison in the other." Example is now the great stimulus.

The Power of Example

All this leads again to the fact that the child, in a most important way during the preadolescent period, mirrors what it sees going on in the family. What the parent *says* has little effect unless it reflects what a parent *does* and *is*. Therefore, a parent dare not be or do what the parent does not want the child to be or do.

The child begins life without knowing what is expected. So the child watches others and tries to do and be what others do and are. All parents have at times been amused at the way the child imitates them and those around them. But it's more than amusing because it becomes a way of life.

Dr. Ralph Heynen in his book, *The Secret of Christian Family Living*, says, "The driving forces of life are emotional, rather than intellectual. Man is a thinking and rational being, but we are not as rational as we think we are . . . A person grows up to be truthful, honest, and generous, not because he is intellectually convinced that such virtues are best for him, but because he has seen these virtues in practices and precepts in his home and cultural setting."[1]

Parents who laugh at speed limits, who "get by" as much as possible in civic and church obligations, can expect no more from their children. What we do as parents speaks louder than what we say. Our day by day examples and family conversations help our children form standards of their own. Parents develop honesty in their children by being honest. Children begin life by being honest—so honest their comments are embarrassing to adults. Along the way they learn deception.

Charlie Shedd illustrated the honesty of a small child in a

story about a mother who worked hard to get an evening meal ready for special guests. It was hot and she was bothered by the heat. Finally when the guests arrived and were seated at the table, the mother called on her small son to ask the blessing. Like any small child he responded by saying, "But Mother, I don't know what to say." The mother replied, "Oh, just pray what you heard me say." The small one bowed his head along with the guests and said, "Oh God, why did I ever invite company on a hot day like this?"

Dr. Kevin Leman in *Making Children Mind Without Losing Your Own* writes about how parents as honest role models teach their children:

1. Through your honesty children learn that it's okay to be less than perfect. Having faults, worries, and failures does not make a parent weird or inferior. On the contrary, it is the strong person who can admit weaknesses.

2. As you model honesty before your child, you have tremendous opportunities to build intimacy and a strong parent-child relationship. By being honest you invite your child into your confidence, into your private world where few people outside the family ever have a chance to observe or listen in. In effect you say to the child, 'I trust you. I value your opinion. I know you are a capable person.'

3. As you model honesty you have opportunity to share your faith in God with your child. You don't have to simply talk about praying to God and trusting God. You can invite your child to actively do these things with you. There is no better approach to reality than that.[2]

Model, Don't Order

In myriad ways the child imitates its parents. Charles, as a young boy, walked pensively with his hands clasped behind his back just as his father did. Imitation is the sincerest form of flattery. It is also the most effective form of learning, especially at this time of life.

Dr. William E. Davis in an article, "Children Need Models To Follow, Not Orders," says that if we consider the amount of time and effort we devote to advising and giving orders to our children, we would be amazed at how little influence we have by *telling* them what to do.

But we can have a profound influence by being a transparent and attractive model to imitate. This means we must be persons with adult integrity. It seems more important to strive for our own self-development, rather than placing priority on self-conscious efforts to mold our children.

Alice V. Keliher writes, "Young children have built-in stethoscopes with which they assess the feelings that surround them. They note well the attitudes and the behavior of their parents and of the other important adults in their lives. They file away these notes, often in deep unconscious storehouses, to guide their responses not only to today's human encounters but also to tomorrow's. Watch them at their housekeeping and folly, or in their improvised dramatics, for clues of what they have learned from the people around them.

"Standards of behavior and courtesy, expressions of respect, demonstration of generosity of spirit, of neighborliness, of decency—these are filed away for further reference. Note the

45

families that generation after generation provide public-spirited citizens. These attitudes do not come by way of the genes and chromosomes."[3]

Respect for others is also developed at home. This attitude grows by observing how parents speak to the salesperson who comes to the house, how they speak to the clerk at the store, or how they speak over the telephone or with a neighbor. Attitudes toward people and issues are reflected in family discussions about others and about the needs of the community and the world.

In addition to the example and teaching of parents, there will always be other significant persons whose lives will be important to the child's development. To make sure the child has the chance to observe and to experience contact with respected and worthy leaders, parents need to consciously take children to meet, hear, and visit with such persons. These contacts are extremely important, particularly during these years of admiration and imitation.

Some years ago a large church body found, in a survey of its ministers, that approximately half of them had decided by the age of eleven years to become ministers. This should not surprise us if we really understand the influence of personalities upon the child during these early years.

Many children choose or feel good about certain vocations early in their lives because of persons in those careers whom they have learned to know and appreciate.

Five of this century's greatest scientists—Edward Teller, father of the hydrogen bomb; Leo Szilard, one of the original atom splitters; Edward Wigner, a famous physicist; Jon Von Newman, a great mathematician; and Theodore Von Karman, the world's most distinguished aeronautical engineer, came from the same town and the same school. All were from Budapest, Hungary, and had one thing in common. They all studied under the same science teacher. Here was a teacher who not only instructed, but inspired. He not only imparted facts, but he instilled a spirit. He not only held a job, but he cast an influence. And it was an influence which caught the admiration of young minds.

Many times in parent-child retreats I've asked participants to reflect on important persons in their lives, persons who were guiding lights and whom they still admire. After inviting them to share the names of these persons with the group and why they were important, I ask, "How old were you when these persons were significant in your life?" Invariably, the age when these persons were significant was in the stage of imitation—middle childhood.

A Sense of Selfhood

During middle childhood the child develops a sense of selfhood. During this time the child feels movement toward adulthood. When this feeling comes, the child wonders what an adult is like and reaches out to imitate adults, particularly parents.

Parents now become flesh and blood heroes with whom the child wants close association. This need is so strong that if parents are not the warm, strong, and needed models, the child will find models elsewhere, and sometimes unacceptable ones. To speak of selfhood means the building of a sense of identity, adequacy, and worth.

Identity

A mother and father tend to play roles that complement each other in their child's developing identity. Identity has to do with "Who am I?", Where am I going?", "What is my purpose for life?", and "Do I feel good with myself as a woman or a man?"

Both parents' goals, senses of direction, and influence, particularly during their child's middle childhood, will have much to do with the identity which that child acquires. Because of the different expectations society places upon women and men, mothers tend to be able to influence their children in particular areas and fathers in others. For example, a mother may express love and support overtly to both her children and her husband. All benefit—her daughters not only receive what she gives, but also observe how she relates, and learn from that. Her sons are likely to develop strong identities, also, as well as the ability to relate kindly and with care to others.

A father's emphasis, on the other hand, tends to be on helping his children set goals and discover a sense of direction. At the same time, the way he shows his love and concern to his wife and children has a major impact on his children's development and their abilities to establish satisfying relationships with others. A sensitive father will focus not only on helping his sons shape their ambitions, but will concentrate equally on helping his daughters explore their strengths and establish their possibilities as they grow.

If both parents love their children as unique persons and distinct personalities, those children will develop strong senses of identity. On the other hand, weak, cold, and aloof, or unprincipled parents produce children who have weak identities and troublesome lives and who often struggle with behaving morally.

A sense of identity is shaped particularly through the period of middle childhood when children are observing and absorbing the characters, conversations, reactions, and actions of those persons to whom they are particularly close, usually their parents and family.

Adequacy

Not only are children forming their identities during this time, they are also developing sensitivity about their adequacy as individuals. The child begins to ask, particularly during middle childhood, "Am I adequate?," "Do I feel strong in my abilities?," and "Am I able to succeed?"

Therefore, the mother, who early in her son's life warmly accepts and lets him help her as she works, builds a sense of self-respect within the boy. When she commends her daughter for doing a job well, and also stands by her in love when she fails, she is building her daughter's sense of adequacy. When a mother and daughter enjoy doing many things together, or when a mother treats her son to a surprise, she is building her children's sense of adequacy for life. The painful phrases of childhood are "You can't do that," "You're too little," and "Get out of my way; I can do it quicker myself." Whether spoken offhand or directly, such statements convey a sense of inadequacy and sap real meaning from a child's life.

The father, who invites his daughter to help him in his work and affirms her at every point possible, builds a sense of adequacy in the girl. When a father plays with his son and doesn't expect perfection, but encourages and supports and affirms him even when he fails, that father gives his children feelings of adequacy to meet life.

On the other hand, attitudes or words of ridicule, sarcasm, or scorn, like, "I can't imagine anyone giving you a job," destroy a child's sense of adequacy. Children who have known such contempt are usually overtaken by feelings of inferiority, the experience which teens describe as their number one problem. A pervasive sense of inadequacy frequently leads to drugs and, in some cases, to suicide, the second highest cause of death among teenagers.

Some time ago I counseled a young man who ran away from home immediately after graduating from high school. He could not wait to leave home. In the counseling sessions he told me, "I never did anything to please my dad." No wonder he wanted to get away. He always felt inadequate around his dad.

Worth

A sense of worth or significance is that internal assurance that children have that they are both valued and valuable, that they exist for a good purpose. A sense of worth is a gift that develops early, particularly during the middle childhood years, in response to the feelings, attitudes, and actions the child senses primarily from parents and teachers.

Feelings of worth arise out of being treated as persons of worth. Sometimes parents treat their own children in ways they would never treat other persons. But when parents say "Excuse me," "I'm sorry," "Please," and "Thank you" to their child, that child feels like a person of worth. When the child is trusted with a surprise or confidentialities, the child feels inner worth. Any of us, but particularly children, grow strong in the areas in which we are praised and encouraged.

A national youth leader told me he could almost always predict the relationship of children and their parents by whether or not the parents introduced their children to him when he was invited into their home.

"My dad always made me feel like I was worth something," a young man told me some time ago. It seemed clear to me why that young man was making a significant contribution in his community.

A man from the Midwest remembered that when he was nine years old, his father had painted on the barn, "Amos Graber and Son." There was no doubt in his mind that he was worth something to his dad. He further recalled that his father and mother never said, "my tractor" or "my car" or "my kitchen" or "my dishes." Instead, they used "our tractor," "our car," "our kitchen," and "our dishes." That spirit of togetherness gave him a sense of worth.

A child's self-worth is also cultivated when she or he is asked for advice and the advice is valued, even though the child is still in middle childhood. A sense of worth is created when a parent has time to listen to a child. It grows when parents recognize the child's unique interests and gifts. It develops when the child is allowed to be an active person in family life.

As a child, one of our three sons had unusual ability and interest in learning how things were made and how they worked. He was skillful in putting things together. When he was perhaps ten years old, we were in need of a garden tractor. My son and I gathered all kinds of information on garden tractors. Then I said to him, "Dave, you've taken interest in this. Why don't you read these materials and then tell me which one you think we should buy?" A few days later Dave returned and said, "Dad, I think this is the one we should get." "Good!" I replied. We purchased that tractor and have never regretted it. Twenty years later it works as good as new in our garden.

"Yes," said a young man, now ready to be married, "I always knew my parents thought I was worth something because they treated me like one of the most important persons around the place."

4.
Development
of the Conscience

One of the most important tasks for children during middle childhood is developing their consciences. Conscience is the ability to distinguish right from wrong. Children learn according to the moral standards of their homes, churches, and communities.

Conscience implies that the child is developing internalized control for right or wrong behavior. As a toddler, a child begins to internalize rules and boundaries, thus forming the seed of a conscience. In middle childhood that seed grows more fully because of the child's rapid cognitive development. This is the time when a child develops the cognitive concepts of fair and unfair and begins to manifest the capacity to understand how another person might feel or think. Moral teaching and example leave a particularly strong impact on a child during middle childhood because of the significant moral development that is also happening during these years.

Since we are not born with consciences, they must instead be acquired, trained, and taught. The responsibility for the content of a child's conscience rests primarily upon the child's parents, although many other influences and agents help set moral standards.

Conscience Takes Shape

Dorothy Corkille Briggs in *Your Child's Self-Esteem* writes: "Most of us want our children to know right from wrong and to be honest, thoughtful and considerate because we are sincerely convinced that is the way to live with others.

"Yet, few of us realize that the conscience only begins to take shape around six. Even then, however, the sense of right and wrong is shaky at best. It needs much outside support from adults. The conscience is made up of the moral standards the child absorbs. What you preach, however, carries far less weight than what you do. The youngster whose parents live with others in a kind, thoughtful, honest way is more than likely to imitate them." [1]

In other words, our children's notions about right and wrong and good and evil are the result of the whole atmosphere they breathe, as well as the instruction they are given. As they grow, these standards become their own. Younger children say something is wrong because they get in trouble for it; middle-age children are able to say something is wrong because it hurts another person's feelings.

Developing a Strong Conscience

To have a strong conscience means to have such a clear idea of what is right or wrong that it controls behavior. Studies show that a child with a strong conscience comes from a family where there are warm, loving, and caring parents. On the other hand, parents who tend to be cold and aloof, as well as overly demanding and meticulous, may cause their child to be weak in confronting temptation when left on his or her own.

When the home is warm and loving, and the parents, though considered strict, exercise a loving response when the child disobeys, the child will seek to measure up to what the parents desire and will be quick to confess wrong. The child prizes the love of its parents. However, when the home is cold and indifferent and the response to wrongdoing does not clearly express love for the child's welfare, the child will be fearful and slow in confessing wrong and will learn to lie in order to protect self.

Strength of conscience depends more on the attachment and identification the child makes with parents, church, school, and community ideals and standards than on a lot of instruction. Here again the child is a great imitator and learns chiefly from example. With whom does the child identify? The child's superego or conscience resides in the child's identity and builds a sense of right and wrong. Since, for example, the boy cannot take his father's place, he can at least seek to be like him, eventually hoping to marry a woman similar to the one his father chose.

The child's identity is shaped by what its parents are and what they expect, rather than by the child's cognitive understanding of all the implications of the parents' choices and behavior. One might say that a child's identification with the significant adults in its life is almost automatic, because that identification emerges before a great deal of the child's own independent judgment does. This attachment to and identification with adults helps give the child an anchor and strengthens the child's becoming a civilized human being with personal control.

The child who does not identify with parents or other significant persons will develop a weak conscience, with weak controls over his or her own behavior. This child is a candidate for juvenile delinquency. Antisocial adolescents and adults come from dysfunctional families in which attachment and connectedness did not occur. Without that attachment, children experience the rules and boundaries that are imposed by others as meaningless, and they have no internal wish to conform to them.

During this stage a child develops the basic disposition which will influence that child's eventual choices of friends, vocation, and life style. The child's capacity in inter-personal relationships and selection of values begins to be established during these years as well.

This is also the time when the child's spiritual beliefs take shape, providing some refuge for the stormy temptations and uncertainty of adolescence.

What About Rules Now?

For children in preadolescence, rules remain important. Witness these children at play. Now they want to play by rules. They refer constantly to the rules of the game. In fact, many middle age children no longer like to play with younger children because they do not keep the rules.

This is also a time when children bargain about keeping the rules. One mother made an agreement with her ten-year-old. "I don't want to be a scolding mother," she said, "so this week I am getting a handful of pennies for us to divide. Any time you hear me scolding, ask me for a penny. But if I find you misbehaving, you must give me a penny. Is it a deal?" Children in the middle age group love such a challenge.

Psychiatrists and family counselors remind us that we do damage to our children if we are too lenient and have too few expectations of them. Children whose parents say they love them too much to punish them are like cars driving down a street without traffic signs. Confused and bewildered, these youngsters may provoke their parents with worse and worse behavior, trying to discover, "If we go far enough wrong, will someone care enough to stop us?"

Our daughter Sandra was chaplain in a girls' prison for a number of years. One of the girls told her, "I never had a curfew. My parents didn't care what I did." Sandra wrote, "At first my young ears heard freedom in Michelle's words. I was remembering all the times as a teenager that I wished my parents wouldn't ask so many questions, wouldn't have so many rules.

"Michelle's 13-year-old eyes, however, did not speak of

57

freedom. She was locked up in a correctional center for juvenile offenders. She said simply, 'I wish they would have loved me enough to make some rules.'"

The sheriff of our county says there are two kinds of youth in trouble. The one is the child who never did anything right. Such a child lacks self-control and is headed toward deep problems. The other kind of youth in trouble is the one who never did anything wrong. Whatever the child did, its parents stuck by it, even lying for the child, never making the child responsible for its actions and behavior. Both kinds of children are confused with weak consciences.

Youngsters themselves ask for stricter discipline. Some years ago the Kansas Council for Children and Youth interviewed high school students about their relationships with their parents. Nearly one-third felt their parents were not strict enough. Several commented that they were confused by the failure of their parents to agree on discipline. "I do a lot of baby-sitting," one girl wrote on her questionnaire, "and I am surprised how many parents allow their small children to make everyone in the house miserable. It's hard for me to believe that a child who is allowed to throw tantrums in order to get her way is going to be more lovable fifteen years from now."

If the home atmosphere is one of love and consistency, the six- to twelve-year-old will begin to demonstrate an active conscience. If obedience is demanded and realized during the early years, the conscience will be developing and deepening, particularly in the middle years.

One girl in trouble with the law said, "If you catch us lying, stealing, or being cruel, get tough. Let us know why what we did was wrong. Impress on us the importance of not repeating such behavior. When we need punishment, dish it out. But let us know you still love us, even though we have let you down. It will make us think twice before we make the same move again."

Proper Motivation for Obedience

Dr. Sheldon Glueck suggests that "unless you build up within the person a stronger motivation for behaving himself than fear, as soon as the officer or father is away, the child will twiddle his thumb at him and go and sin some more." Strong motivations for right behavior must be built into the character of the child. This is done by setting a good example for the child and by steadfastly loving the child.

A survey of ten thousand delinquents showed that they had one thing in common—all had experienced a lack of affection. A child who receives warm affection responds with love and obedience. Urban Steinmetz comments, "I am beginning to believe that a parent can't make too many mistakes if love continues to come through."

Consistent love—the Senate Subcommittee on Juvenile Delinquency emphasized that children need to know they can count on their parents' love. The report says that the lines of character and self-control are erected in the individual, if at all, by definite rules administered fairly and firmly. This is done through love and praise for right actions and through withdrawal of approval (not love) for violations. When children know only approval or neglect, there is no dynamic force through which they can create or identify with their parents' standards of behavior, life, and conduct.

Clara Lambert writes, "Your child wants rules, laws, and

regulations, but they like the 'rubber band' type which can be stretched a little but not broken. You cannot afford to be spineless or afraid of your children. You must know how to compromise graciously, be firm without rancor, be fair, and even look the other way sometimes to sidestep an important issue."[2]

The Goal

Of course the ultimate purpose of training is to help the child become an independent, thinking person who will be able to face life and decide moral issues. An encouraging word is extremely important when the child does choose the good. By a word of criticism or comfort, the child's spirit can be stifled or strengthened.

Many parents are guilty of injustice against their children by offering only correction and rebuke. Conversely, when the child feels enveloped in love and warmed with trust, the child is in optimum circumstances for making right choices. The home is the place to help children develop these inner responses and strengths so that they can learn to fly.

When parents are realistic about their own mistakes at home, they help their children to be realistic in evaluating themselves. As parents we may correct or punish our children too severely or cut them off with an impatient answer. When we apologize, children may recover from the hurt more quickly than we recover from the guilt over what we have done.

Gibson Winters suggests that parents can build a whole dimension of life for their children by confessing their own injustices and asking for forgiveness. Such experiences help children see that forgiveness is part of the very fabric of human relationships. They learn that a transgression does not end the relationship. They learn that transgressions can be opportunities for deeper personal relationships. They learn that you do not have to be perfect to be accepted and loved.

During a counseling session a father told about how he had spoken too severely to his eleven-year-old and, to his dismay, had cut off communication between them. I proposed that he apologize to his son, ask for forgiveness, and wait to see what would happen. When he apologized, reported the father at the next counseling session, his son came to him, threw his arms around him, and said, "I really love you Dad."

Spiritual Dimensions

It is during the middle childhood years that the spiritual world either takes on real meaning and importance to the child, or is seen as irrelevant and undeserving of any authentic commitment. This is determined largely, of course, by what the child observes of its parents' sincerity and seriousness. Xavier Lefebyre and Louis Perin in *Bringing Your Child To God* say: "Nothing impresses a child so much as the regard parents and teachers have for everything which concerns God and the respect with which they perform their religious acts, and usually the child will experience real joy in imitating them in this." [3]

Respect for the spiritual is shown in the tone of one's voice, in pictures and reading material in the home, in the care and seriousness with which parents take part in religious services and ceremonies.

When we speak of spiritual truth, the child should receive the impression that we are revealing something of great value to us. When we speak of God, children should sense respect and honor; when we pray or read the Scripture, children should realize the importance these have for us.

Even more important are the ways we parents model love, trust, caring, faith in God, and happiness in our relationships. When children see the place the spiritual has in their parents' lives, they are inclined to seek it as well. When children see parents happy in their spiritual lives, they receive a deep and indelible impression.

Albert Schweitzer, the great scholar, scientist, and philosopher, gave tribute to the piety of his parents and their deep devotion to God for his own spiritual resources and commitment. It was as he watched his parents in their daily lives at home, in their faithfulness to the church, in their deep reverence in worship, and in their speech concerning spiritual things, that he felt deeply within the reality of God.

Three Parables

Some years ago I found these parables.

I took a little child's hand in mind. The child and I were to walk together for a while. I was to lead the child to the Father. It was a task that overcame me, so awful was the responsibility. I talked to the little child only of the Father. I painted the sternness of the Father's face, were the child to displease Him. We walked under tall trees. I said the Father had power to send them crashing down, struck by His thunderbolt. We walked in the sunshine. I told the child of the greatness of the Father who made the burning, bla. sun.

And one twilight we met the Father. The child hid behind me; the child was afraid; the child would not look up at the loving face. The child remembered my picture and would not put a hand in the Father's hand. I was between the child and the Father. I wondered. I had been so conscientious, so serious.

* * *

I took the little child's hand in mine. I was to lead the child to the Father. I felt burdened by the multitude of things I was to teach. We did not ramble. We hastened on from spot to spot. At one moment we compared the leaves of the trees; in the next we examined a bird's nest. While the child was questioning me about it, I hurried the child away to chase a butterfly. If the child happened to fall asleep, I wakened the child lest my little one should miss something I wished my child to see. We spoke of the Father often and rapidly. I poured into the child's ears all the stories the child ought to know. But we were interrupted often by the wind blowing, of which we must speak; by the coming out of the stars, which we must need study; by the gurgling brook, which we must trace to its source.

And then in the twilight we met the Father. The child merely glanced at Him. The Father stretched out His hand, but the child was not interested enough to take it. Feverish spots burned on the child's cheeks. Dropping exhausted to the ground, the child fell asleep. Again I was between the child and the Father. I wondered. I had taught my child so many things.

* * *

I took a little child's hand in mine to lead the child to the Father. My heart was full of gratitude for the glad privilege. We walked slowly. I suited my steps to the short steps of the child. We spoke of the things the child noticed.

Sometimes it was one of the Father's birds; we watched it build a nest, and we saw the eggs that it laid. We wondered later at the care it gave its young.

Sometimes we picked the Father's flowers, stroked their soft petals and loved their bright colors. Often we told stories of the Father. I told them to the child, and the child told them to me. We told them, the child and I, over and over again. Sometimes we stopped to rest, leaning against the Father's trees, letting His air cool our brows and never speaking.

And then in the twilight we met the Father. The child's eyes shone. The child looked up lovingly, trustingly, eagerly, into the Father's face, and the child put a hand into the Father's hand. I was, for the moment, forgotten. I was content.[4]

5.
Development of Dependability

Responsibility and dependability rank high among the traits we desire in our children. These are traits which are valued at home, school, church, and in our communities. Dependability means to take the appropriate action or to make the proper response on one's own, out of an inner urge or compulsion. How much dependability and responsibility should we expect of our children during their various phases of development, particularly in middle childhood?

Being dependable is exhibited in the regular routine of tasks, as well as in emergencies. It is a learned attitude; it is the result of learning to consider others. Becoming dependable also goes hand in hand with developing a conscience and learning to discern what is best in the long run, not just what is pleasing at the moment. Dependability takes into account the welfare of others as well as one's self. It is learning to assume one's share of the tasks which need to be done.

How then do we parents encourage responsibility and dependability in our children?

Encourage the Child's Own Resourcefulness

If when we notice a child's own resourcefulness we encourage the child, the child will grow in dependability and responsibility. Billy, ten years old, built a magazine rack for his room. When he showed his dad the rack and how he had arranged his magazines, Dad sincerely praised Billy for the project and complimented him for what he had done. Billy immediately planned another project to keep his room in better shape—a shoe holder which he had seen pictured and thought would make a good project. Billy, through all of this, became more responsible for his room.

Trust with Small Projects Early

Maria is almost three years old. Her job each day is to feed the family dog. While I was visiting in her home, Maria's mother said, "Oh, Maria, it's time to feed Tipper." Proudly Maria went to the cupboard, filled the dish to the right level, and took it to the porch. Maria's mother, while this was going on, was telling me how good a job Maria does and that she knows exactly how much to feed Tipper. Maria is learning dependability in small projects she can handle. An important part of the process is the encouragement she is receiving from her mother. A young child who is trusted and invited to carry through on small projects soon learns the satisfaction of doing a job well.

Include your child in planning a family picnic or trip. Give the child specific responsibilities to help make it a success. Then be sure to express your appreciation to the child for helping. In addition to enjoying a good family time, your child will have grown significantly in dependability through the experience. When the child is given opportunities to do things for neighbors and friends, the child feels the satisfaction which such helping brings and finds joy in being needed. If doing what should be done brings recognition or praise for a well done task or a more pleasant relationship with others, the child will learn to be dependable.

Catching Their Parents' Spirit

Parents' example is crucial. When parents demonstrate that caring for others is a part of adult behavior, the child catches the idea. The child absorbs the spirit of its parents and other significant adults in its life. This is especially true for the child in the middle childhood stage of imitation, who is particularly likely to copy parental behavior and the behavior and feelings of close friends of the family.

When the family is concerned for persons beyond itself, the child is quick to sense these feelings and to pick up concerns and obligations for others. Self-indulgent parents do not raise children who sense a responsibility for others. When a father announces to his family, "No TV tonight for me; I promised to help Jim move," he has done more for his child's sense of responsibility for others than a dozen Sunday sermons.

When a child sees parents make right choices, even when it's costly, the child learns much about moral responsibility. The same is true in smaller matters. If parents hang up their coats when they enter the house, the child is more likely to assume responsibility in this area.

One father, when backing out of a parking space, put a slight scratch on an adjacent car. No one saw the accident except his six-year-old son seated beside him. The father got out of the car and placed a note on the windshield of the car with his name, address, and telephone number. He explained to his small son what he did and that he wanted to see that the car of the other person was fixed. That son, even after thirty years, remembers that incident with great clarity and still tells what a sense of responsibility he learned when he was six years old.

Point Out a Child's Dependability

Because children tend to live up to the image they feel others have of them, we strengthen our children's trustworthiness when we let them know we depend on them. Although the child will sometimes fail, we need to tell the child specifically, "I can depend on you" and "I know you are the kind of person who will follow through on this." This adds to the child's self-respect and demonstrates that everybody benefits when one is responsible.

Appreciation is the key which unlocks a helpful spirit in the home. We parents are prone to think that our children's work is our due. Furthermore, it is often easier for us to correct and criticize than to commend. But if we want to teach our children to work, we must celebrate the child's successes. Jane Grossman writes in *Life With Family* that "celebrating success is important. We should register our pleasure and satisfaction when a son or daughter shows improvement in a heretofore difficult course, when work is well done."

Expressions of appreciation encourage a child to help at home. When the child first picks something up from the floor, stimulate the child's spirit of helpfulness with a smile and thank-you. Use compliments generously to call out the child's best. Parents who practice praising their child for work well done will find the child living up to his or her reputation. They will also find the child more ready to respond positively in other areas of living.

In his book, *How To Help Your Child Grow Up,* Angelo Patri says that just as every artist needs an audience and perishes without one, so every child who does something of achievement needs to be praised. The young performer is inspired by the acceptance and approval of adults whom the child longs to please.

Perhaps it seems inconsequential to say to a young son, "That was a good job you did," when he fixes a doorknob or puts a new washer in the faucet. But it isn't. It may seem insignificant to tell a teenage daughter, "I feel safe when you are taking care of your brother." But such statements call forth an attitude of even greater responsibility. When Dad asks, "Mother, did you see Danny help me clean the garage today?" he is instilling in Danny the satisfaction of achievement and the joy of joining another in work.

69

Regular Chores

Giving a child regular chores in line with the child's competence helps to build dependability. Young children can help empty waste baskets, carry out the garbage, and sweep the garage. Too often we "efficient" parents tell our small children to get out of the way, and then expect them later to respond readily to our assignments.

Parents are often tempted to say to their small children who want to help with whatever is being done, "I can do this more quickly myself, so please go and play." Those same parents are inclined to say to their teens, "If you want to live here, you ought to do something to help around the place." It is easy to miss the early opportunities for helping children develop dependability. But it is extremely difficult to have them learn it later. Parents will discover that children learn best if they are first given responsibilities that relate as closely as possible to their interests. Adults must also keep in mind the fact that if children are overwhelmed by a responsibility, they will lose the whole point of the experience.

Shared Experiences

Use stories to reinforce your child's learning of responsibility. Encourage your children to read stories of other children who exercised courage, resourcefulness, dependability, and steadfastness in situations similar to your children's own experiences. Such accounts are particularly appealing to children in middle childhood. Call attention to happenings in your community in which these traits are displayed. It makes these qualities seem believable and attainable. Nothing, of course, impresses a child more than its parents telling stories from their own lives and practicing these traits themselves. Parents sharing from their own experiences is one of the prime ways of teaching values to children in their middle years.

Beware Of Unreasonable Demands

Many children are drawn by the challenge to tackle new, and more difficult, adult responsibilities. Parents, at those times, need to be discerning and watchful that they are not allowing their children to make unreasonable choices with far-reaching results. Parents can, wittingly or unwittingly, present their children with too much responsibility related to decisions which parents still need to make. If parents are not alert or do not intervene, their children may become afraid and shrink from assuming appropriate responsibility at that time or even in the future. Offering children the opportunity to carry responsibilities in keeping with their ages and abilities cultivates their senses of reliability and responsibility.

Sometimes a child's interest in doing a good job is dampened by an adult placing too high standards on the task. The child who cannot meet those standards develops feelings of inferiority and may retreat into the child's own world. Parents and adults need to find ways to give suggestions for improvement while also giving many words of encouragement.

Organized Groups Can Help

Being part of an organized group can enhance a child's sense of responsibility and develop the child's dependability. In clubs, athletic teams, or performing groups, a child can assume a share in what is decided and learn to be dependable in carrying out her or his own part through attending meetings, rehearsals, or practice sessions, and doing special projects. In a group, a child senses special obligation to classmates or team members and begins to understand what it means to be responsible in the wider community.

We parents need to remember that our own interests in being helpful and responsible, as well as in solving problems, grow chiefly through being part of families in which mutual assistance is practiced. Children likewise understand what they see practiced.

The Place of Praise

Always encourage your child, no matter the size of his or her success. Every child thrives on approval, success, and achievement. Beware of criticism. During the middle years especially, negative criticism can create a hesitant, ill-at-ease child who draws back from any kind of action or decision. On the other hand, praise encourages the child to develop abilities and dependability because every child has a deep desire to please. William Jones wrote, "The deepest principle of human nature is the craving to be appreciated." Never is this more true than in middle childhood.

When we praise a child, we encourage that child to move

closer to the estimate we have of the child's potential. As J.W. Goethe explained, "In praising or loving a child, we love and praise, not that which is, but that which we hope for." And August W. Hare said the same thing this way: "The praises of others may be used in teaching us, not what we are, but what we ought to be." The art of praising precedes the fine art of pleasing.

Praising a child about anything you can find to compliment does multitudes more to encourage that child than a dozen scoldings for not doing something right. The Scriptures give clear, sound advice when they state in the positive, "Train up a child in the way the child should go." (Most children would be reared almost perfectly if it said instead, "Train up a child in the way the child should not go"!) We are inclined to say, "Don't do that" or "Don't say that." There are times when negatives are needed, to be sure. But for direction and growth the child needs training in what *should* be done and said. We need to accentuate the positive. One compliment to a child for keeping the bedroom or playroom clean and attractive does more than many reprimands.

Will Sessions commented, "I would bestow praise. If the youngster blew a horn I would try to find at least one note that sounded good to my ear and I would say a sincere word about it. If the school theme was to my liking, I would say so, hoping that it would get a good grade when it is turned in. If his choice of shirt or tie, or socks or shoes, or any other thing met my liking, I would be vocal." No other thing so effectively encourages a child to love life or to seek accomplishment as sincere praise.

In one experiment psychologists selected an average group of students, but told their teachers these students were highly intelligent. By the end of the year, because of the attitude and enthusiasm of their teachers, these students' performances surpassed the most brilliant group in the school.

Give the Child a Choice

To build dependability, a child needs opportunities to choose. Children who are allowed a choice of tasks gain a sense of ownership and grow in responsibility for their tasks. Ask for and respect a child's decisions whenever possible. Personality develops by making choices. A child will not venture an opinion if that child's opinions were knocked down again and again in the past. To be disregarded emotionally can leave more long-term damage than to be knocked down physically.

Whenever we treat our children with respect, we make them persons who are respectable. When we treat them with love, we make them lovable. And when we honor them, we make them honorable. These are laws of life.

6.
The Demise of Childhood

I was seated in the third row watching a wrestling tournament. The tournament was provided by the community during the summer months for grade-school students. The boys had practiced for some weeks, and now they were in the finals. Parents and friends were present. Excitement was high.

A little fellow, perhaps nine years old, had just finished and lost his match. Dejectedly he walked over and sat beside his father in front of me. To my dismay the father began to deride and criticize, even curse, his small son for his failure to win.

His son sat silent and still as he suffered not only what was a humiliating defeat before so many adults, but worse, a pitiless onslaught by his own father in front of others. He suffered all this from a supposedly grown-up man who felt the most important thing was winning, from a parent who found his own ego hurt or threatened when his son failed to win.

What does an incident like this say? It is only one illustration of our failure to let children be children. Even more, it is an example of how we parents seek to find our own fulfillment in our children. Children in our society are under tremendous pressure to succeed beyond their years. And the success aimed for is usually that of the parents' rather than that of the children.

Eberhard Arnold, in his excellent book *Children's Education in Community: The Basis of Bruderhof Education,* writes, "If we exploit the child's ability to devote himself to something great by binding him to ourselves and to our little ego. . . or to selfish gratification, we are corrupting the child and destroying his childlike spirit." [1]

Let Children Be Children

Children have the right to be immature and to be permitted to grow up gradually. Our children need from us the opportunity for experiences that they are capable of handling, our assurance that we are there to encourage them, and our acceptance of their efforts without belittling them.

The soaring suicide rate among adolescents confirms that childhood is not a happy time. Dr. E. James Anthony, a St. Louis psychoanalyst, points out that today's children appear to be born old. Their faces are cynical as they enter adolescence. The reasons, Anthony says, are that we as parents expect too much too soon. Children are under sustained pressure.

Dr. James Dobson, assistant professor of pediatrics at the University of Southern California School of Medicine and director of behavior research, Division of Child Development for Children's Hospital of Los Angeles, writes in *Hide or Seek*, "The current epidemic of self-doubt has resulted from a totally unjust and unnecessary system of evaluating human worth now prevalent in our society." He devotes two chapters to an analysis of the false values on which self-esteem so often depends in our culture. The two he discusses in depth are beauty and intelligence. Beauty and brains seem to be prime requisites if one is to be of any worth.

According to Martha Weinman Lear, author of *The Child Worshipers*, the younger generation is our most reliable status symbol. The hopes, dreams, and ambitions of the entire family sometimes rest on the shoulders of an immature child. We place our children in atmospheres of such fierce competition that they are threatened with severe damage.

In an article in *U.S. Catholic*, "Let My Children Grow," Ned O'Gorman writes, "I know a boy of six who wrote a poem about his perception of life, and one line in it was: 'childhood is a closed door.' " O' Gorman guesses that when the boy is older he may add this explanation: "Childhood is a closed door. My parents and teachers closed it." [2]

Armin Grams in *The Christian Encounters Changes in Family Life* says that, "paradoxically, the child-centered home has brought with it unprecedented pressures for children to stop being children. We have taken childhood away from children, not only by watching them too closely and focusing on them excessively. We are also unwilling to permit them their time in growing up."[3]

Unreal and Hurtful

Because we do not see childhood as a legitimate phase of life itself, and because we as parents feel the need to find our success in our children, we do many ridiculous things. At three months we buy toys parents like to play with. An electric train is purchased and set up by parents whose child still wants to stack blocks. A tricycle stands riderless with the driver in diapers. We dress five-year-olds in caps and gowns for kindergarten graduation. A little fellow recently said, "I think it is bad I graduated because I can't even read."

Little girls who would choose to play with dolls are driven downtown for dancing lessons. We pair off boys and girls in first grade. We elect them to class offices before they have an idea what it means. We form committees and teach them to vie for positions before they know what a committee is. We dress them like adults. And some mothers are proud when their eleven- and twelve-year-old daughters are popular with the boys. "Little Miss" and beauty contests are held, paying the wrong kind of attention to children.

In sports we expect children to play like professionals before they have hips big enough to hold up their uniforms and before they have hands large enough to handle a ball and glove. And while the game is going on, parents sit on the sidelines harassing the player who makes a mistake, applauding the one who excels, and yelling for victory at all costs. Some time ago a Little League coach told me that parents should not be allowed to come to the games. Adults spoil the fun. They will not permit children to enjoy the game as children.

Little Leagues often deny the child the right to be a child. First, they create too much pressure to produce while adults cheer or jeer, depending on their assessment of how "adult" their children's performance is. Second, the whole setting is exclusive—only the good players play, and the creativity of learning through failure in a loving atmosphere is missing. The game must be played according to adult rules and supervised by adult coaches and umpires.

Pressure at Other Places

Parents drive children to despair in their demands that they make good grades. It is not uncommon for children to say that they cheated because of pressure from parents.

Even in the church, mothers and fathers sometimes feel the church is neglecting, even rejecting, them as parents if the church bulletin or an announcement misses calling attention to the accomplishments of their child. If the church fails to use their child prodigy in singing or performing otherwise, some parents are hurt. Our precious children are too often put forward to place feathers in our own caps.

Our vocabulary says we are geared not to children, but to their later years. We speak of pre-school, pre-adolescent, pre-teens, and junior high school. The pre-adolescent bra, for example, has good sales.

In an article, "No Furniture Till Forty," Phyllis Naylor says

79

we should have the type of furniture in our homes that allows children freedom to play. If we continually tell children to take their hands off things, it is likely that we have our priorities in the wrong place. Things, rather than persons, predominate in our thinking.

Marilyn Bonham in *Laughter and Tears of Children* points out that parents and society contribute to precocious sexuality. Some people permit, if not encourage, their nine- and ten-year-olds to date. Too many twelve-year-olds are provoked into sexual identification that is far too premature and probably not of the child's choosing in the first place. So also, Bonham points out, "The premature use of lipstick, nail polish, teased hair, and high heels is psychologically unsound and denies the child the all-too-brief innocence of childhood." [4]

Some fathers push their sons into situations of masculine independence, thus hampering the emotional growth of children who are still floundering about in search of themselves. Behavioral scientists point out that toy manufacturers and other business interests are successfully changing the nature of children's play. Instead of three- and four-year-olds playing with stuffed animals or dolls, trucks, or model cars, they are pushed to fantasize about life as an adolescent. Take the Barbie doll, with its focus on sex and materialism, as an example.

Because of such pressures, psychiatrists warn that children are breaking down emotionally in increasing numbers and at younger and younger ages. Our society's great drive for superiority results in persons of all ages experiencing feelings of inferiority. And feelings of inferiority make up a chief emotional problem of teenagers today, a problem that drives many to depend on drinking and drugs.

At least two causes create these feelings of inferiority. We adults pass on to our children the great stress we carry to be superior. Yet few of us can be superior in *one* thing. What chance do our children really have to be superior in *many* things? Another reason for the inferiority complex shadowing many teenagers today is the permissiveness in many homes that forces youth to make decisions they are not prepared to make. In many cases, they simply lack experience and knowledge. When parents do not stand by to assist their youth in making life decisions and when parents have no clear code of conduct themselves, they are bound to build feelings of insecurity in their children.

Why All the Pressure?

Why do parents put so much pressure on their children to excel in beauty and brains, in sports and showmanship, and in dressing and performing beyond their age?

Is it that the childlike qualities of imperfection, curiosity, honesty, and naiveté are threatening to parents? Is it that parents are so insecure that any failure on the part of their child threatens them?

Is it that we build our own egos from our children? Do we strive to succeed through what our children accomplish? Perhaps we have failed in accomplishing what we desire, so we must have children who succeed at all costs. Seeing our children in proper focus is difficult if we are unhappy in our own lives.

Psychiatrist Bernard Trossman has said that perhaps the most pernicious parental attitude is the spoken or unspoken communication that the child must provide meaning for its parents' empty lives.

When a mother pushes a daughter into beauty contests, or a dad pressures his son into sports or some academic endeavor, or parents place the birthday picture of their two-year-old in the newspaper, are they concerned for the child, or are they only shoring up their own egos?

Might the pressure we at times put on our children be the result of our having set impossible standards of achievement for ourselves? Are we consequently making excessive demands on our children? Are we burdening our children with our expectations for their achievement because of our own feelings of inadequacy?

Reaching for a Remedy

Sometimes parents feel forced to allow their children to enter roles prematurely because of the standards others set. Gene Church Schultz, a teacher and an astute observer of youth, wrote an article in which she states that young people "need parents who are strong enough to stem the rising tide of growing up too soon." She describes the difficulty of being the "heavy" in the drama of growing up. The older youngsters become, the louder they may cry that "everybody else is doing it." Parties last too long, boy-girl affairs start before children are ready, and all kinds of grown-up situations are forced on adolescents. She points out that it is very easy to let children follow the practice of the crowd, to bend with the prevailing wind, to say, "Oh, O suppose so—this time."

"However," says teacher Schultz, "there is another

consideration. When parents band together in organizations like the Parents' League or even informal groups, the position of each parent is strengthened. Usually other parents share our concern. They would like to say 'no,' but lack the muscle to enforce it. A single phone call to another pair of parents may bring in reinforcements."

Examine Family Values

We must examine our family values. What are our real concerns? If our values are to get ahead materially, be popular, and receive applause, then we will go on using our children, and we will place primary emphasis on *things* rather than on *persons*. To see our children clearly we must examine our own values, goals, and attitudes and look at ourselves as parents.

In an article, "Who Is Pressuring Pre-schoolers?," James L. Hymes, Jr. writes, "Parents are trapped by their love for their children. They don't pressure them because they are callous or careless; parents pressure because they care. They want their youngsters to have the best, to be the best, to know the best, to do the best. Their fond wishes and their aspirations, their hopes and their dreams, not to mention their own pressures, drive them—and they drive their youngsters." [6]

However, steady pressure strains life and presents the constant possibility of failure for the child. It takes the joy out of living. Steady pressure is bound to strike at personal worth and dignity. It says, "You don't measure up." It leads to the child's rejection later of even good standards, when the child refuses to accept parental pressure during adolescence or upon leaving home for college or work.

But as parents we do not need to stay trapped in driving either ourselves or our children. We can stand back and consider what counts most in life, what is most important. We can look at what we really want. We do not need to make our children pawns of our unfilled personal needs or dreams.

We must stop robbing our children of happiness by forcing them into roles for which they are not yet ready. Those parents who allow for creativity on the part of their children, who stand beside them when they do their best—or when they fail—will have children who will develop confidence and trust, children who will find life an open, happy experience. Children need understanding as they use their imaginations, curiosities, and wonder to find their own fulfillment.

This does not mean that we parents should drop all aspirations for our children and do nothing. It does not mean that we let our children do as they will. It means, rather, that we look closely at our own motives and aspirations and recognize them for what they are. It means that we consider carefully what most helps our children to develop into free, independent, and responsible adults.

When loving parents spend time with their child, they are doing the best teaching. Skills grow best in good, happy relationships. When a family spends time listening, answering questions, working, and playing together, a lot of good can happen. Parents who share story times, game times, and talking times with their children open all kinds of doors for their children to happily walk through rather than be pushed through. And when children walk through doors out of their own desire, they participate as happy, responsible, and patient persons, rather than pressured individuals fulfilling roles for which they are not ready.

Dr. Bernie Wiebe writes how, through a mistake made on a citizens' list in Houston, Texas, a two-year-old child received summons for jury duty. Said Wiebe, "To me that seems like a double ironic error. First, here we again see a child cast into the role of an adult. But it should perhaps remind us that a child is the legitimate judge before which civilization should be tested." [6]

* * *

Father Forgets: (a final word by W. Livingston Larned)

Listen, son: I am saying this as you lie asleep, one little paw crumpled under your cheek and the blond curls stickily wet on your damp forehead. I have stolen into your room alone. Just a few minutes ago as I sat reading my paper in the library, a stifling wave of remorse swept over me. Guiltily I came to your bedside.

These are the things I was thinking, son: I had been cross to you. I scolded you as you were dressing for school because you gave your face merely a dab with a wet towel. I took you to task for not cleaning your shoes. I called out angrily when you threw some of your things on the floor.

At breakfast I found fault, too. You spilled things. You gulped down your food. You put your elbows on the table. You spread your butter too thick on your bread. And as you started off to play and I made for my train, you turned and waved a hand and called, "Good-bye, Daddy!" and I frowned, and said in reply, "Hold your shoulders back!"

Then it began all over again in the late afternoon. As I came up the road I spied you, down on your knees, playing marbles. There were holes in your stockings. I humiliated you before your boy friends by marching you ahead of me to the house. Stockings were expensive—and if you had to buy them you would be careful! Imagine that, son, from a father!

Do you remember, later, when I was reading in the library, how you came in, timidly, with a sort of hurt look in your eyes? When I glanced up over my paper, impatient at the interruption, you hesitated at the door. "What is it you want?" I snapped.

You said nothing, but ran across in one tempestuous plunge, and threw your arms around my neck and kissed me, and your small arms tightened with an affection that God had set blooming in your heart and which even neglect could not wither. And then you were gone, pattering up the stairs.

Well, son, it was shortly afterward that my paper slipped from my hands and a terrible sickening fear came over me. What has habit been doing to me? The habit of finding fault, of reprimanding—this was my reward to you for being a boy. It was not that I did not love you. It was that I expected too much of you. I was measuring you by the yardstick of my own years.

And there was so much that was good and fine and true in your character. The little heart of you was as big as the dawn itself over the wide hills. This was shown by your spontaneous impulse to rush in and kiss me good-night. Nothing else matters tonight, son. I have come to your bedside in the darkness, and I have knelt there ashamed!

It is a feeble atonement; I know you would not understand these things if I told them to you during your waking hours. But tomorrow I will be a real daddy! I will chum with you, and suffer when you suffer, and laugh when you laugh. I will bite my tongue when impatient words come. I will keep saying as if it were ritual: "He is nothing but a boy—a little boy!"

I am afraid I have visualized you as a man. Yet as I see you now, son, crumpled and weary in your cot, I see that you are still a baby. Yesterday you were in your mother's arms, your head on her shoulder. I have asked too much, too much.

Questions for Further Discussion

 ## Chapter I (pages 9-22)

1. Review the "last things" discussed in this chapter and give illustrations which you have from your own experience.

2. The change from preadolescence to adolescence is an abrupt one, or so it seems. Suddenly relationships which seemed serene become strained. Do you agree that relationships in adolescence depend a great deal on relationships during "middlescence"?

3. "Talking our values" is the way one father describes his teaching. This father feels that, if parents daily discuss openly and honestly their beliefs with their middle-childhood offspring, those children will hear and learn the values of life. How can such family discussions be vital?

4. What other important "last things" do you see as you think of the middle years?

Chapter 2 *(pages 23-40)*

1. What other characteristics of middle childhood come to your mind?

2. As mentioned in the Introduction, this book does not discuss the physical development of the child. Are there aspects of this part of a child's growth which you would like to discuss or have someone else explain?

3. Some might question whether children in middle childhood love to please parents and other adults. How do you evaluate this statement?

4. List practical ways parents can demonstrate love and affection to their children. If possible, read Ross Campbell's book *How To Really Love Your Child*.

5. Discuss "hidden hostility" and its effect on the family, particularly children. How do you feel about the child hearing or seeing parents disagree?

6. Think back and share what an encouraging word meant in your life.

7. "Doing things together" gives a sense of belonging. What do you remember doing together as a family, and how old were you when you did these things?

Chapter 3 (*page 41-52*)

1. During the first five years of life, a child is primarily guided through regulation. The child who does not learn rules early will probably always struggle or search for boundaries. During middle childhood the primary way of guidance is through imitation. Discuss the difference and the implications.

2. What is the place of regulation during middle childhood?

3. We want each of our children to have a good sense of selfhood. Discuss the ways to help that happen suggested in this chapter and add additional ideas. What characterizes a poor sense of self-worth?

4. Are there particular ways in which a single parent can help her or his child develop both a strong sense of identity and adequacy? Can that parent build contacts with relatives, adult family friends, or clubs who represent, in some part, the same gender as the missing parent?

5. Take time to think of your own sense of adequacy and worth. From whom did you get or fail to get help in developing these?

Chapter 4 (pages 49-60)

1. What do you think accounts for the differences between a strong and a weak conscience? How is each developed?

2. What do you think of the sheriff's evaluation of youth in trouble with the law?

3. Do you agree that many youth want firmer discipline? Are parents afraid of their children, or why do parents shy away from expecting obedience?

4. Do you agree that the middle years are the time to put more and more responsibility for discipline into the hands of the child so that the child will assume personal and proper responsibility later on? How is this done? Could children be part of establishing family rules and the consequences for broken rules?

5. What does the child learn when the parents confess their own failures?

6. Discuss motivations for proper behavior. List what is necessary for building a strong conscience.

Chapter 5 (pages 65-74)

1. Dependability and confidence in doing a job well can develop early in children. Because both take time to teach, we parents are inclined to tell our little ones to get out of our way.   During middle childhood children like to be part of doing things. List ways of encouraging this inborn trait.

2. How do we stifle a child's desire to help?

3. All of us feel good when we are affirmed. The ability to affirm or praise our children is a real test of our own self-worth. What do you feel best about in your own life? Why?

4. If you listed one thing which is most important in developing dependability, what would it be?

Chapter 6 (pages 75-88)

1. Do you sense that we in our society have a critical problem in allowing children to be children?

2. What do we mean by the "child-centered home," and what are its dangers?

3. What are proper and improper expectations to have for children?

4. Do you agree that the great drive for superiority builds all kinds of feelings of inferiority?

5. Discuss the ego trips we parents take related to our children's performances.

6. How can we buck the pressure put on parents to have their children succeed?

Endnotes

Chapter 2, "Characteristics of Middle Childhood," pages 23-40.

[1] Evelyn Millis Duvall, *Handbook for Parents* (Nashville, TN: Broadman Press, 1974), p. 13.

Chapter 3, "Guided by Imitation," pages 41-52.

[1] Ralph Heynen, *The Secret of Christian Family Living* (Grand Rapids, MI: Baker Book House, 1969). p. 57.

[2] Kevin Leman, *Making Children Mind Without Losing Yours* (Old Tappan, NJ: Fleming H. Revell Co., 1987), p.46.

[3] Alice V. Keliher, "What Should Parents Teach?" *Christian Living* (December, 1968). pp. 26-27.

Chapter 4, "Development of the Conscience," pages 53-64.

[1] Dorothy Corkille Briggs, *Your Child and Self-Esteem* (Garden City, NY: Doubleday & Co., 1970) p. 145.

[2] Clara Lambert, *Understanding Your Child From Six to Twelve,* Public Affairs Pamphlet Number 144 (Public Affairs Committee, Inc., 1948), p.31.

[3] Xavier Lefebre and Louis Perin, *Bringing Your Child to God* (New York, NY: P. J. Kennedy annd Sons, 1963), p. 25.

[4] John M. Drescher, *Seven Things Children Need* (Scottdale, PA: Herald Press, 1988) pp. 126-128.

Chapter 6, "The Demise of Childhood," pages 75-88.

[1] Eberhard Arnold, *Children's Education in Community: The Basis of Bruderhof Education* (Rifton, NY: Plough Publishing House, 1967). p. 21.

[2] Ned O'Gorman, "Let My Children Grow," *U.S. Catholic.*

[3] Armin Grams, *The Christian Encounters Changes in Family Life* (St. Louis, MO: Concordia Publishing House, 1968), p. 47.

[4] Marilyn M. Bonham, *Laughter and Tears of Children* (New York, NY: Macmillan Publishing Co., Inc., 1968).

[5] James L. Hymes, Jr., "Who Is Pressuring Pre-schoolers," *Christian Living* (February, 1969), p.28.

[6] Bernie Wiebe, "Let Children be Children," *Christian Living.*

[7] W. Livingston Larned as quoted by John M. Drescher in *What Should Parents Expect?* (Nashville, TN: Abingdon, 1980), pp. 11-13.

About the Author

John M. Drescher, Harrisonburg, Virginia, was born and grew up near Lancaster, Pennsylvania. He is married to Betty Keener and they are parents of five grown children.

He has authored 28 books among which are *Seven Things Children Need, If I Were Starting My Family Again, Now Is the Time to Love, Spirit Fruit, When You Think You Are in Love, Meditations for the Newly Married, Why I Am a Conscientious Objector,* and *If We Were Starting Our Marriage Again.*

Drescher has written for more than 100 different magazines and journals. His books have appeared in 10 different languages.

He has spoken to numerous conventions, retreats, and seminars—particularly in the area of family life.

Great ideas—for a great need! *101 Ways to Romance Your Marriage* is packed with powerful and playful ways to keep the passion in your marriage!

—Pam and Bill Farrell, authors
Men Are Like Waffles,
Women Are Like Spaghetti

101 Ways to Romance Your Marriage will thrill your heart, put your romance into high gear, and create vibrations of love. Every married person should have this fabulous book on the coffee table to refer to constantly, and every single person should keep it handy for the future. You will love this book!

—Kathy Collard Miller,
speaker and author
Princess to Princess

Here's proof that marital love isn't monotonous. This book is packed with inspiration for intimacy, sizzle for sex, and poetry for passion.

—Deb Strubel, associate agent
BigScore Productions
Lancaster, PA

When we are first married, romance comes naturally. However as the years go by and life gets in the way, loving our mate extravagantly becomes passé. I am glad to have contributed to this clever collection of ideas and inspiration to bring spice and surprise back to marriage.

—Marita Littauer, speaker and author
president, CLASServices Inc.

Not since Marabel Morgan's mega-bestseller, *Total Woman,* has a book come along that ignites the fires of romance. Debra White Smith has written a masterpiece on love at its best. This book is guaranteed to rekindle the fires of romance in many homes.

—Stan Toler, author
Minute Motivator series